Original title:
The Island Song

Copyright © 2025 Creative Arts Management OÜ
All rights reserved.

Author: Fiona Harrington
ISBN HARDBACK: 978-1-80581-649-2
ISBN PAPERBACK: 978-1-80581-176-3
ISBN EBOOK: 978-1-80581-649-2

Dreams in the Driftwood Dance

Driftwood swinging by the brine,
Seagulls cluck, they think they rhyme.
Crabs in sandals, doing a jig,
While fish all laugh—oh what a gig!

Sunburnt pirates on parade,
Wobbling boats, no shade, no trade.
They toast to seas with mugs of foam,
While jellyfish crash like a cartoon dome!

Rhythms of the Endless Horizon

Fins and flippers in the mix,
Dolphins toss some ocean tricks.
Surfboards dance like clumsy seals,
Waves can't help but break their wheels.

Sandcastles rise, then tumble down,
Beachball kings who wear a crown.
Sunscreen got them all a-glow,
While sunburnt noses steal the show!

Solstice Serenade by the Sea

Underneath the coconut spree,
Crabs hold hands for a fruity tea.
Lobsters strum on shells so bright,
Sipping sunset, feeling light.

Starfish clapping in their chairs,
Breezy hair and salty flares.
As night descends, they start to croon,
With moonlit whispers and a tune!

Tidepool Reverie

Tiny worlds in shallow pools,
Wiggly worms and squishy schools.
Starfish sculptors make a mess,
While seaweed plays dress to impress.

Clams play poker on the sand,
Laughing loudly, isn't it grand?
Tidepools dance to rhythms fine,
With knee-deep laughter and a brine.

Ocean's Enigmatic Verse

Beneath the waves, a fish so spry,
Wearing a hat, oh my, oh my!
He dances quick with a flip and a twirl,
Singing sweetly, giving pearls a whirl.

A crab in shades, he struts with flair,
Cracking jokes, without a care.
While seahorses spin in a comical race,
With grins so wide, they light up the place.

Octopus Chef, the master of stew,
Whips up some dishes, oh so blue!
He serves up laughs with every delight,
For bubbles and giggles make the meal bright.

As tides start to laugh and seagulls play,
Fish throw a party that lasts all day.
With bubbles of joy all around the shore,
Life undersea is never a bore!

Portholes to Paradise

Through portholes wide, the sights unfold,
A mermaid dances, her tale retold.
With a wink and a splash, she invites a tune,
Singing to crabs that are chasing the moon.

A dolphin dives in with a flip and a giggle,
Leading the way with a splashy wiggle.
While a turtle brings snacks, a pizza to share,
His friends all shout, "More cheese! We declare!"

The pirate's parrot reads jokes to the crowd,
A chorus of laughter, vibrant and loud.
While squids juggle pearls, as they flail,
A sport for the ages, a slippery tale.

In currents of joy where the sun shines bright,
The ocean sings songs of pure delight.
With whims of the sea, let's join in the cheer,
For laughter and fun, we hold so dear!

Soliloquy of the Surf

Waves crash and whisper a tale,
Seagulls dive down without fail.
Sandcastles stand, a proud sight,
As kids chase their dreams in the light.

Crabs in a hurry, sideways they go,
Wiggling their claws, putting on a show.
Beachballs are bouncing, kids run amok,
While sunscreen fights off the dreaded sun shock.

Cool drinks in hand, too sweet to share,
A pineapple hat? Why, who wouldn't dare?
Laughter erupts, it's contagious and bright,
As we dance with the tide under soft, starry light.

Harbors of Forgotten Wishes

In a cove where dreams like shells lay,
Forgotten hopes drift in salty spray.
Turtles wear sunglasses, quite a cool sight,
Making wishes on waves that dance with delight.

An octopus with a hat made of foam,
Guides weary sailors back to their home.
Mermaids giggle, tossing their hair,
As seaweed floats like a grin in the air.

The waves sing lullabies, a soft serenade,
To fish in a school doing the cha-cha parade.
In this harbor, where laughter is law,
Every wish comes true with a twinkling jaw.

Breathless Horizon

The sun dips low with a golden grin,
While boats race off, let the fun begin!
With flip-flops flying and laughter that soars,
Chasing horizons, we hunt for the shores.

Clouds puff like marshmallows in the sky,
While dolphins leap up, oh my, oh my!
A kite tangled in palm trees so high,
As beachgoers whisper, "How did that fly?"

The ocean hums tunes of a playful breeze,
Tickling our toes and teasing our knees.
A horizon that smiles with every wave's sway,
Reveals silly secrets of a sun-kissed play.

Chorus of the Caribbean

Under a sun where the coconuts sway,
Swaying to rhythms that dance through the day.
Drums beat like hearts, and feet tap in time,
As jellyfish jig to an old sailor's rhyme.

The parrot squawks jokes over piña coladas,
While tourists compete for the best limbo stances.
Flip, flop, and giggle, we're all in the game,
As laughter resounds, we forget our name.

Sea turtles toast to a spectacular feast,
While crabs have a dance-off, the fun never ceased.
In this garden where colors brightly blend,
The chorus of joy knows no end.

Lullabies of the Lagoon

In the lagoon, the frogs croon,
With croaks that echo past the moon.
A fish flips out, lands in a hat,
And giggles swim around like that.

Sand crabs dance with sideways pride,
While sea turtles roll like they've got a ride.
Banana peels, our sliding path,
We slip and slide, oh what a laugh!

The coconut tree starts to sway,
As parrots mimic what we say.
A pelican tries to steal our fries,
But ends up wearing them as a prize!

Swaying in night's gentle embrace,
We join the tide in a silly race.
With laughter bright as the stars above,
The lagoon hums with a joy we love.

Dances on the Coral

Under the waves, the fish do twirl,
While the sea urchins begin to whirl.
Octopus in sneakers, what a sight,
Bright colors dance in the pale moonlight.

Starfish clapping with flippers wide,
The eels all wiggle, full of pride.
While crabs march in their finest shoes,
Stomping out rhythms, they can't lose!

A dolphin steals the scene with grace,
Winking at the jellyfish with a bubbly face.
They all join hands, no one falls,
As the coral reef rings with joyful calls.

With laughter soaring where waves break free,
Nothing but silliness in the sea.
As bubbles rise and the music swells,
We dance with fish—oh can't you tell?

Serenity's Serenade

In a hammock made of seaweed thread,
Sunbeams wiggle, as if they're fed.
The seashells try to sing along,
But only echo a funny gong.

A dolphin sings to the crabs nearby,
With a voice that's more silly than shy.
The seagulls swoop, attempt to dance,
While a fish spins like it's in a trance.

As sea foam giggles, tickling toes,
Sandcastles laugh at the waves that close.
With every splash, our worries fade,
In this balmy haven, a jest parade.

As day turns soft with twilight hues,
We share our laughs on sunset views.
With serenity wrapped in jolly cheer,
The ocean whispers, "Stay right here!"

Breeze-Kissed Dreams

The breeze delivers whispers sweet,
Of coconut cakes and tasty treats.
Kites made of fish scale float so high,
While seagulls pass, waving goodbye.

Clouds play peek-a-boo with the sun,
As the island laughs, all in good fun.
Waves tickle toes that dance on sand,
Life in this place is simply grand!

We chart out maps in a playful way,
With treasure marked on every bay.
A parrot argues over the prize,
While shenanigans bloom before our eyes.

At dusk, the stars tie laughter's knot,
In this haven of joy, we find our spot.
With breeze-kissed dreams and hearts so light,
We celebrate the wonders of the night!

Harmony on Forgotten Waves

Seagulls squawk with glee,
Shells giggle on the shore,
Crabs dance in their suits,
While sandcastles start to snore.

Waves whisper silly jokes,
As flip-flops take a flight,
Beach balls start to tumble,
Under the pale moonlight.

Palm trees sway and laugh,
Their coconuts conspire,
A surfboard's getting jealous,
Of mermaids who aspire.

So raise your drink and cheer,
For laughter fills the air,
On forgotten waves we sing,
A party without care.

Lullaby of Coastal Nights

Underneath the starry skies,
The crabs hold their dance-off,
While starfish judge with silly eyes,
And seagulls scoff and scoff.

The waves sing sleepy tunes,
With bubbles in the mix,
Sand dunes wear cozy blankets,
In a rhythm that just clicks.

Shells share stories of the day,
Of swimmers going 'oops',
And dolphins doing belly flops,
While joining in the whoops.

As night drapes in a blanket,
The moon joins in the fun,
Coastal nights of laughter,
Where silliness is spun.

Rhapsody of Sunlit Sands

Sunshine spills a golden hue,
As kids skip and trip along,
With sunscreen blobs like missing shoes,
A rhapsody in throng.

Buckets brimmed with sand and dreams,
Each wave a tickled toe,
A giggle here, a wobble there,
With laughter's joyful flow.

Kites soar high, then tumble down,
Like clowns upon the breeze,
The beach turns into circus rounds,
As nature aims to tease.

So join the cheerful melody,
With towels that play peek-a-boo,
A sunlit stage for all to see,
With quirks in every view.

Overture of the Ocean's Heart

Beneath the waves, a treasure gleams,
In fishy tales of gold,
The octopus spins yarns so grand,
While jellyfish unfold.

With surfboards making goofy sounds,
And laughter riding high,
A sandpiper joins in the fun,
As kites just flutter by.

The breeze plays tunes on seashells bright,
A concert to behold,
With crabs in tuxedos doing jigs,
While ocean rolls in bold.

So dance along the ocean's beat,
With humor on the tide,
An overture of silly dreams,
Adventure as our guide.

Tidewater Tales of Old

There once was a crab with a knack,
He danced on the sand with a clack.
The seagulls looked down,
In hats made of brown,
As he jived with the waves on the track.

A fish with a tail so long,
Joined in on the silly song.
They swirled with the tide,
In a whirl, oh so wide,
Creating a splash where they throng.

The old sailor grinned with delight,
He watched the strange dance at night.
With a pint in his fist,
He couldn't resist,
To join in the joyful sight.

So if you find crabs in a line,
Just laugh, and give them a sign.
For in this great choir,
Their spirits won't tire,
At the tidewater's edge, they entwine.

Symphony of Sundrenched Solitude

On a beach where the sun likes to play,
A whale told a story one day.
He hummed a wise tune,
To the stars, the bright moon,
While the dolphins just flipped in ballet.

There lounged a fine turtle named Joe,
Who took life exceedingly slow.
With a wink and a grin,
He just tucked his chin,
And said, "Why bother with go?"

The gulls did a tap dance for fun,
While the tide pulled the shells on the run.
With a plop and a crash,
They made quite a splash,
In a show that just couldn't be done.

So if ever you feel quite alone,
Seek out the laughter you've known.
The sand and the waves,
Have music that saves,
A symphony bright as a stone.

Whispers of the Tide

In the hush of the twilight's embrace,
Fishes conspired with glee on their race.
With bubbles and quips,
And some funny flips,
They painted the bright ocean space.

A clam claimed the title of king,
With a crown made of seaweed and bling.
But the tide had its say,
As it washed him away,
So he danced to a new tune of swing.

The sand formed a jester's great hat,
As a crab found a way to chit-chat.
With each quirky line,
He made humor divine,
While the sea joined his laugh, how about that?

So listen when waters collide,
For stories and whispers abide.
In the dance of the blue,
There's laughter for you,
In the rhythm of tides, come inside.

Melodies of Sand and Sea

A wacky old pelican flew,
With a shoe on his head—it was true!
He croaked out a tune,
'Neath the light of the moon,
As the crabs chimed in with their glue.

Shells clinked like glasses of cheer,
Celebrating the fact we were here.
With a flip of a fin,
And a laugh in the din,
Ocean's joy always seems near.

A starfish declared he could dance,
With moves that just seemed to enhance.
He twirled on a wave,
And the beach was his stage,
While the seagulls all joined in the chance.

So gather around for a spree,
Where the sand and the sea sing with glee.
With laughter so bright,
It's a marvelous sight,
In melodies shared, come and see!

Lull from the Lagoon

A frog croaks a tune, oh so loud,
While fish do a jig in the murky shroud.
Crabs dance in circles, all dressed in flair,
While seagulls squawk jokes, without a care.

Splashing all around, the laughter will soar,
As turtles join in, then they laugh even more.
Coconuts wobble, they fall with a thud,
And everyone giggles, laughing in mud.

The sun dips low, painting skies so bright,
Even the sand thinks it's a delight.
Breezes carry whispers of giggles and cheer,
As night drifts in, but the fun's still near.

So come all you friends, let's sing along,
In the land of the silly, we all belong.
With every last wave, let worries flee,
For laughter and joy are the key to be free.

Serenade of the Dunes

A lizard in shades strums on a string,
While errant sand flies knock on a wing.
A crab with a banjo, strumming it right,
Makes all of us giggle, oh what a sight!

The dunes roll on, like waves of delight,
As the sun bakes the day, oh what a delight!
Grasshoppers hop, creating the beat,
While skittering bugs join in with their feet.

Seagulls are jesters, flapping and dive,
While cacti join in, they give a high five.
The wind carries whispers of humor and cheer,
As friends gather 'round to chortle and jeer.

With shadows that dance on this sandy floor,
We laugh and we sing, who could want more?
If you hear the dunes, just know it's a blast,
With funny little tunes, they'll hold you fast.

Nautical Whispers at Dusk

Sailboats are prancing on waves of gold,
While parrot birds squawk tales, daring and bold.
Fish in tuxedos, they swim with such flair,
In a comedy show, they make quite the pair.

The moon starts to climb, all white and round,
While lanterns bob gently, would make a fine sound.
Octopuses juggle, with tricks that surprise,
As dolphins blow bubbles, they spin and they rise.

Crabs in their suits glide across the deck,
Turning somersaults, what a funny wreck!
The sea joins in laughter, waves chuckle and roll,
As night falls, a giggle tide sweeps through the shoal.

So gather your friends, and dance on the shore,
For nautical whispers will keep you wanting more.
With smiles and the stars, brightening the night,
We'll share all our stories till morning's first light.

Harmony of Lost Horizons

At the edge of the sea, where the sun meets the blue,
A pelican dives for a snack, who knew?
The shrimp wear top hats, they're ready to jam,
As they shuffle and shimmy, oh what a slam!

The horizon plays tricks, tilting this way,
As a wave-washed surfboard rolls in with a sway.
Dolphins are dancing, with spins and a grin,
While starfish tell tales of where they've been.

Coconut palms sway, they wear leafy crowns,
Their whispers of humor spread chuckles around.
Dunes giggle softly, with sand in your toes,
As laughter erupts, wherever it flows.

So come take a stroll, let your worries all flee,
In this harmony, laughter flows wild and free.
With twilight as our curtain, we quirk and we shine,
In this land of mirth, our souls intertwine.

Shadows Beneath the Surface

Beneath the waves, a fish did dance,
He thought he'd try a funny prance.
But lacking fins, he took a fall,
And now he sings, that fishy ball!

A crab decided to join the show,
With claws that waved in a silly flow.
Together they laughed, they gave a cheer,
While other fish just rolled in fear!

A seagull swooped, oh what a sight!
It crashed headfirst, a comedic flight.
The ocean echoed with giggly sound,
As shadows beneath wiggled around.

Now every day they gather near,
To dance and laugh without a fear.
The ocean knows how to have fun,
A party where no one's ever done!

Embrace of the Ocean

In waters deep, a whale wore shades,
He strutted past, under sun's glades.
His friends just splashed and had a blast,
Laughing at silly seaweed cast.

A dolphin flipped, a cheeky grin,
He juggled shells with a clever spin.
The octopus clapped, all eyes set wide,
As sea creatures joined in, laughing with pride.

A sunken ship became a stage,
For all the fish, who felt the rage.
They danced like crazy, a fishy spree,
In the embrace of the ocean, pure glee!

So, if you dive, don't swim alone,
Join in the fun, make it your own!
For ocean joy is never short,
And laughter is the sea's finest sport!

Solstice on the Shoreline

On the shoreline, a seal with flair,
Wore a top hat, danced without a care.
He flipped and slid, a coastal king,
While crabs played drums, oh what a swing!

The tides applauded with snappy claps,
As seagulls cheered, in stylish caps.
They rapped and chirped, such a delight,
Celebrating Solstice under moonlight.

The sand joined in, with a soft, warm grin,
As footprints formed a goofy spin.
A wind gusted by, playing a tune,
And the shoreline danced beneath the moon!

Gather around for this joyful chance,
To wiggle and wiggle, it's your last dance!
For the solstice shines with a gleeful call,
Let's party and laugh, let's have a ball!

Twilight's Nautical Lull

As twilight glimmers on ocean's face,
A starfish yawned, took his place.
He whispered secrets to the tide,
Making sure his friends abide.

A pelican perched, quite the sight,
Held fishy gossip by moonlight.
With wings spread wide, he told a joke,
While jellyfish giggled, and quite awoke.

The lighthouse blinked with a silly grin,
Guiding the night, letting fun begin.
Waves whispered softly, they danced along,
In the lull of twilight, hearts sang the song.

So if you wander where waters play,
Listen closely, laugh the night away.
For twilight's charm brings joy to the bay,
And nautical lullabies brighten the day!

Treasure Beneath the Waves

Pirate dreams of gold and fame,
They duck and dodge, can't play the game.
With maps so old, they always fail,
To find the loot or even sail.

They dig in sand, they dig in mud,
For shiny coins, or just a dud.
Adventure calls, but what a laugh,
They trip on boats and spill their staff.

A treasure chest? Oh, what a tease!
It's filled with socks, not jewelry, please!
They strain and scratch, searching with greed,
But find only crabs and seaweed.

Their laughter rings over waves so bright,
As gulls swoop down, what a funny sight!
With every splash, their joy ignites,
In goofy quests on warm moonlit nights.

Jasmine Breeze at Dusk

Jasmine scents dance in the air,
The breeze tosses knots in their hair.
While sipping drinks with silly straws,
They giggle loud, breaking all laws.

A toucan sings a wacky tune,
While monkeys mime beneath the moon.
They joined the chorus, hopping about,
With flip-flops flapping, oh what a shout!

The sunset paints their faces bright,
As shadows play a comic fight.
They trip on tales of crazy things,
And laugh at life as it joyfully swings.

The jasmine breeze whispers low,
With stories of mischief, fun and woe.
They dance like fools under pastel skies,
With silly grins and sparkling eyes.

Sails Against the Sunset

Sails billow high on a puff of air,
The crew all giggle without a care.
In mismatched outfits, they catch the breeze,
While seagulls squawk in raucous tease.

A captain shouts, "All hands on deck!"
But spills his drink, what the heck!
They fumble ropes with hapless grace,
As laughter fills the open space.

They steer the ship, it turns askew,
Chasing the sunset, not much they knew.
With every wave, they tumble and sway,
But laugh it off, it's all in play.

The stars come out, their guide so bright,
As they toast to woes and silly delight.
With sails flapping in perfect disarray,
They sing a tune, the night takes sway.

Songbirds of the Ocean's Edge

Songbirds chatter in feathery glee,
Perched on driftwood, as happy as can be.
They chirp their tales of grand escapades,
While waves bring secrets from ocean glades.

A crab joins in with a clumsy dance,
In the sea foam, it takes a chance.
The birds all chuckle, flapping their wings,
As they mimic the crab's silly flings.

A fish jumps high, just out of view,
Creating ripples that sparkle and cue.
The birds all cheer, "Do it again!"
Believing the ocean, their funny friend.

With sunset colors painting the sky,
They fill the air with their jubilant cry.
As day turns to night, they nestle down,
The songbirds of laughter, the jesters of town.

Echoing through the Palms

In the shade where coconuts sway,
A parrot squawks in a comical way.
The crabs do a dance, oh what a sight,
While tourists trip over in pure delight.

Laughter rises like waves on the shore,
As locals tell tales of the infamous boar.
Drinks in hand, they all start to cheer,
Sipping on concoctions with a hint of beer.

The beach ball rolls, just out of reach,
A kid trips, flops, such a funny breach.
Seagulls steal fries, they seem so sly,
As sunburned tourists just laugh and cry.

At sundown the night brings a fiesta scene,
With toc-toc drums and dancers so keen.
Sand-covered feet and a glow of the moon,
Echoing laughter will end way too soon.

Melodic Mournings at Dusk

As the sun bows down, the sky's a mess,
Crickets croon, oh, what a guess!
The fish jump high, as if they sing,
A turtle claps, oh what a fling!

With every swell, the wave brings a joke,
A coconut lands with a thud and a poke.
Alligators grin, with their toothy charms,
While a dog swims by, seeking safe arms.

The boatman yells, 'Don't mind the splash!'
While kids laugh and make a silly clash.
The evening winds bring giggles alive,
As everyone here seems to thrive.

With stars peeking out, the night comes alive,
Dancing shadows under the moon's bright dive.
Melodies mingle, a cacophony wild,
As even the crabs join in, all beguiled.

Aria of the Starry Bay

Under a cloak of twinkling lights,
A boat floats by, full of merry sights.
Fishy friends try a splashy ballet,
While they sing to the moon, in a flirty display.

Frogs on a lily-pad make a critter choir,
Their croaks mix well with the night's require.
An octopus plays a slippery sax,
As sails flap in rhythm, like wavy wax.

The beach goes wild with a crumby delight,
Chasing each other till they take flight.
With laughter so loud, they leap to the bay,
Life's just a giggle in this funny play.

Stars wink above, they join in the game,
Creating a night that's hard to tame.
The aria floats on the breezy tide,
In this world of fun, where joy's our guide.

Dance of the Wandering Winds

The winds come twirling, with giggles and sighs,
Whipping up sand in a playful disguise.
Palm trees wave with their leafy big arms,
As children chase after the breeze's charms.

Seashells clatter, a rhythm ensues,
Skimming the shoreline in colorful hues.
With every whoosh, a new joke takes flight,
As critters join in for a carnival night.

An old dog barks at a fluttering kite,
While grandpa hums, his voice full of light.
Everyone spins in this whimsical game,
As the winds laugh along, never quite tame.

The night whispers secrets with breezy grace,
With laughter echoing in this wondrous space.
Together they sway, as the stars play along,
In the frolicsome dance of this one joyous song.

Echoes of Distant Shores

A crab in a hat dances by,
Waving his claws to the sky.
Seagulls laugh as they swoop low,
Chasing the sand with a silly show.

The waves whisper secrets to the breeze,
Tickling the toes of the tall palm trees.
A sunburned tourist sings off-key,
While fish giggle at his jubilee.

Umbrellas flip in the wind with glee,
As children shout, "Come and swim with me!"
A beach ball flies over a sunhat's crown,
Who knew the sea could be such a clown?

The tide keeps rhythm, a goofy beat,
As shells conspire on the sandy seat.
In the end, laughter echoes galore,
Where silly tales roam from shore to shore.

Whispers of Untamed Waters

A dolphin prances in a fishy trance,
While starfish plot their grand romance.
Mermaids giggle, tossing seaweed strands,
As crabs hold a banquet on soft, yellow sands.

The ocean sings songs of bright escapades,
Shells acting silly in sequined parades.
Jellyfish twirl in a dance so grand,
With every splash echoing in the sand.

Frogs in flip-flops leap to the beat,
While sea turtles race to their own happy feet.
Unexpected guests, a flock of pink quirks,
Joined by the tide in this ocean of perks.

The water winks at the bright open sky,
As clouds drift by, whispering a high.
In this playful realm, joy finds no flaws,
Where laughter's the music, and fun is the cause.

Serenade of Sandy Dreams

Beneath a sun that's a bit too bold,
A pirate's hat made of waffle cone gold.
Sandcastles melt, a royal disgrace,
As pails and shovels take up the race.

Flip-flops go flying in a comic spree,
Dancing along with a wild bumblebee.
Children with squirt guns engage in a fight,
Creating a splash that feels just right.

While sunburned folks lament their plight,
A clam in a tux gives everyone a fright.
Seashells hum tunes of forgotten fame,
As tides chase dreams while they play their game.

Each grain of sand holds a giggle or two,
As laughter pours forth like morning dew.
In the corners of joy, mischief does gleam,
Welcome to the world of sandy dreams.

Ballad of the Tide's Embrace

The tide rolls in with a comical grin,
Hitching a ride with a jet ski spin.
Flip-flops and sunscreen collide at the bay,
As seagulls squawk in a raucous array.

A fish in a tutu hops on the shore,
While sandpipers scurry, and seabirds soar.
Balloons float high in a colorful dance,
As kids wiggle their toes, lost in a trance.

A pelican steals snacks right off the mat,
As a beach ball bounces high like a cat.
Sandcastles watch with a regal flair,
Chasing away troubles, evoking a fair.

From dawn until dusk, the fun won't cease,
Where laughter flourishes and worries release.
The tide whispers tales of jubilant grace,
Embracing us all in its playful embrace.

Tales of the Azure Horizon

On a shore where coconuts sway,
A crab wore a hat, bright and gray.
He danced with the breeze, quite the sight,
Claiming the day as his own delight.

The seagulls squawked with comic flair,
While fish swam in circles, unaware.
A pirate parrot, bold and spry,
Searched for treasure while sipping chai.

A turtle flipped burgers on the sand,
Crafting meals that were truly unplanned.
With laughter so loud, they could not resist,
Join the feast, you wouldn't want to miss!

As sunset spread colors of gold,
The tales of the day were eagerly told.
With a wink and a chuckle, they all lay down,
In the humor of the sea, none wore a frown.

Reflections in the Water

The fisherman tossed his line with a cheer,
But caught a boot that was far from mere.
He pondered a fish that had gotten away,
While the boot just floated, 'Come fish, let's play!'

The frogs on the lily pads wore little hats,
With humor that rivaled mischievous cats.
They croaked tunes that could make anyone smile,
Even the fish joined in with their own style.

A duck with a quack so delightfully loud,
Waddled about, drawing quite the crowd.
He laughed with the breeze, as if to say,
"Life is a joke, come laugh with me, hey!"

By the pond where thoughts drift and wander,
Reflections of laughter cause us to ponder.
In a world where the silly and whimsical play,
Every ripple brings joy to the end of the day.

Songs of the Distant Isles

A ship made of wood, and a crew of dreams,
Danced to the rhythm of odd little themes.
The captain wore shoes that were far too big,
While a monkey on board thought he'd be the gig.

They sailed past an octopus juggling well,
Who dropped a few shells with a loud 'Oops!' yell.
The fish in the sea had a party so fine,
Disco lights twinkled, like stars they would shine.

A flute-playing crab and a bass-playing star,
Brought together a jam, it went quite bizarre.
They sang of the tales, of pirates and seas,
Where laughter was bound by the rustling leaves.

In faraway isles where the tall palm trees sway,
The humor of travel would guide their way.
With memories of laughter that echo and bloom,
They'd sail back again to continue the tune.

Harmonies of Coastal Night

The moon winks at waves in a game of peek,
While crickets play tunes that make us all speak.
A mongoose in shades croons a soft lullaby,
As stars giggle low and let dreams fly high.

The breeze tells stories of beaches and fun,
Of sandcastle kingdoms where everyone's won.
A firefly leads a dance with delight,
Float on, you bright wonders, through the soft night.

A clam with a grin on the edge of the shore,
Shouted, "More jokes!" as he wanted some more.
With laughter around, it turned cool into warm,
Where harmony thrived in a lively swarm.

So let's sip on the laughter of coastal delight,
And dance with the shadows till morning's first light.
In the heart of the night, with humor as guide,
We'll sing through the moments where joy will abide.

Chasing the Distant Horizon

On a rubber boat we sail,
With a crew of ducks, we'll prevail.
Chasing sunbeams in a race,
Shouting 'Catch us if you can!' with grace.

Fish are leaping, quite a sight,
Waving fins with sheer delight.
Seagulls squawk and dive around,
Yet our snacks always hit the ground.

Across the waves we skip and hop,
But oh dear! Someone's flip-flop!
Lost among the ocean's charm,
Who needs shoes? We've got our palms.

So here we drift, a merry band,
With sunburns forming on each hand.
Chasing joy as we explore,
And leaving all our cares on shore.

Whispers of the Coral Caves

Underwater secrets tease and taunt,
With fish that twirl in a shimmering font.
Bubbles rise with stories told,
Of mermaids dancing, brave and bold.

Crabs in shoes, they scuttle past,
Each with tales, a treasure amassed.
Jellyfish float in a jelly trance,
As we join in their silken dance.

A starfish nods, with a wink so sly,
While wise old turtles swim by.
'Join us here for a snack,' they say,
But finger sandwiches float away.

In every crevice, laughter sings,
Coral castles and seaweed rings.
We'll explore until the tide's reprieve,
With fishy giggles we believe.

Drifting with the Current

On a log we sail, like a trusty boat,
With snacks that simply never float.
Each wave a chuckle, each splash a song,
As the current pulls us right along.

Turtles laugh, 'You've got no helm!'
While jellybeans ours truly overwhelm.
Muddy feet and tangled hair,
Become our fashion, we just don't care!

The sun's our guide, with a wink and cheer,
While seagulls provide the sound effects here.
With snacks as our compass, we glide and spin,
Each misadventure makes us grin.

At the end of the day, we bask in bliss,
Who knew drifting could feel like this?
Every twirl spins a laugh or two,
With salty tales to share anew.

Essence of the Coastal Dawn

The sun peeks over like an eager child,
Painting the skies with colors wild.
Crickets settle into sleepy hush,
While the waves start their morning rush.

Coffee grounds spill like morning fun,
As we lounge under the warming sun.
Sandcastles rise, then swiftly fall,
A high tide's giggle, a nature call.

Waves bring shells and a craggy rock,
Seagulls waiting for a clock to tick-tock.
Frolicking crabs, they strut their moves,
Proving that dancing is the way to groove.

The scent of salt, mixed with delight,
As laughter echoes, day turns to night.
With each dawn's charm, we'll sing this song,
In coastal laughter, where we belong.

Breath of the Salted Air

The seagulls laugh, they dive and swoop,
While tourists slip, they fall, they whoop.
A crab in shorts struts on the shore,
Pretending to be a dancing chore.

Waves tickle toes and splash a grin,
A kite takes flight, the wind's best friend.
Flip-flops flying, hats off the head,
A picnic ruin, who needs that bread?

Sunshine pops like fizzy drinks,
Sandy sandwiches, who even thinks?
Salt left behind on every chair,
Who cares? We're free, with salty air!

Sunscreen battles, each smeared arm,
The seagull's stealing our lunch, no harm!
In this funny patch of beach and fun,
Laughter echoes, we've just begun.

Footprints in the Sand

Footprints wander, zigzag wide,
Chasing crabs as they swiftly hide.
In a race with waves, we dance along,
Expecting tides to sing our song.

A flip from a friend, a splash so bright,
Turns the fun day into sheer delight.
Slippers lost, laughter found,
Each step a tale on the sandy ground.

The tide comes in, our prints erased,
But in our hearts, they still have space.
Seagulls giggle overhead, oh what a sight,
As we chase our dreams into the night!

Stumbling over shells, what a trip!
Don't mind the sand, let laughter slip.
In the sun's embrace, we take a stand,
Just leaving silly footprints in the sand.

Aerial Dance of the Pelicans

Oh pelicans, with wings so wide,
Gliding through clouds as if they glide.
They drop like stones, but what a show,
Dining in style, oh, to and fro.

Splashing down with a honk and flair,
Those funny birds just don't care.
Fumbling fish with gaping mouths,
Laughing at currents, doing their rounds.

They half-pull off, it's quite a sight,
Strutting their stuff, they own the night.
Each flap is funny, they float with grace,
In this comedy of wings, they find their place.

So here's to the flocks, the dance in the sky,
The blend of chaos, oh my, oh my!
With every dip, they brighten the shore,
Aerial antics we can't help but adore.

Lanterns of the Southern Cross

Beneath the stars, we hum and sway,
Lanterns bobbing in the bay.
Driftwood fire, oh what a glow,
As shadows dance, our laughter flows.

Old tales spun with cheeky grins,
As the night deepens, the fun begins.
Glow sticks waving, a neon crew,
Who knew camping could feel so new?

The Southern Cross shines overhead,
Making promises, like fairies spread.
Marshmallows toasted, sticky delight,
Ghost stories told with squeals of fright.

Riddles and giggles, the ocean sings,
With every spark, our joy takes wings.
Here on this shore, together we'll stay,
Under lanterns bright, we dance the night away.

Chants Beneath the Canopy

In the shade of bright green leaves,
Laughter echoes, mischief weaves.
Monkeys swing with goofy grace,
Chasing shadows in this place.

Parrots gossip, colors clash,
Dancing feathers, a silly flash.
Crickets join with their loud refrain,
Making music, the joy uncontained.

Turtles waddle with a smile,
Strolling slowly, taking a while.
Coconuts fall with a splendid thud,
Silly moments in the sand and mud.

Beneath the sun, we sing and play,
Life's a joke on this bright day.
Giggles ring from tree to shore,
In this laughter, we all want more.

Melodies of the Coral Reefs

In waters clear, fish dance and twirl,
Tickling sea anemones, giving a whirl.
Clownfish crack jokes, a colorful crew,
In their wild world, always something new.

Starfish lounge, don't lift a limb,
Floats and waves sing their whimsical hymn.
Shark swims by, wearing a grin,
In the ocean's chaos, they secretly win.

The octopus juggles shells on parade,
With a wink and a flip, antics cascade.
Coral gardens bloom with a laugh,
In this splash zone, we share the craft.

A dolphin's laugh echoes so bright,
Joining the chorus, a playful sight.
Underwater whimsies fill the sea,
Where even the tides giggle, wild and free.

Soliloquy of Salt and Sea

Waves whisper secrets, so silly and sweet,
Telling of sailors who danced on their feet.
Seagulls giggle, beak in the air,
As antics unfold without a care.

Sandcastles crumble with great delight,
As children run from the tide in flight.
Buckets and shovels become the kings,
While whales hum soft, their odd little sings.

The salty breeze ticks every nose,
Bringing laughter wherever it blows.
Crabs doing crabwalks, what a sight!
Life's a party in the warm sunlight.

Under moonbeams, the sea has a tale,
Of joyful splashes and fun without fail.
Join in the chorus, let spirits soar,
In this salty serenade, we can't ignore.

Songs from the Seashell's Heart

Seashells whisper, secrets they keep,
Songs of the ocean, echoes so deep.
With a twist and a turn, they sing out loud,
Bringing laughter to the listening crowd.

Crabs in tuxedos tap-dance with flair,
While snails glide slowly without a care.
That wiry eel with a twinkle in eye,
Cracks jokes in bubbles that float to the sky.

The jellyfish sway, a graceful ballet,
In their gooey skirts, they frolic and play.
Starfish add in with starry-eyed glee,
As the ocean hums its quirky decree.

Beneath the surface, life thrives and plays,
With each little sound, the ocean conveys.
In shells made of laughter, joy finds its way,
Singing together, come join the ballet!

Heartstrings of the Tide

Waves are dancing, they shimmy and sway,
They tickle the sand, then frolic away.
A crab in a tux, with a shell for a hat,
Chases a seagull who's stealing his snack.

A dolphin with swagger, jumps through the air,
Singing sweet tunes to the blissful sea fair.
Fishermen below think they've found him a mate,
Turns out, it's just a fish with a date!

Jellyfish glide by, like ghosts in the night,
Just trying their best not to cause a fright.
Their wobbly dance is quite comical still,
As they float through the water, it's quite the thrill.

The breeze tells a secret, a joke from the tide,
The rocks start to chuckle, they can't seem to hide.
Laughter erupts from the shells on the shore,
Who knew that the ocean could make us adore?

Celestial Waves

Stars in the sky giggle at night,
While waves below watch, sparkling bright.
A fish with a crown waves hello to the moon,
He swears he's a prince, making quite the tune.

Squids in a circus, their ink flying high,
As octopuses juggle, they catch every sigh.
A whale with a look, so hilarious and grand,
Tells tales of his travels across the highland.

The sea turtles waddle, their flippers in sway,
Practicing dance moves while laughing away.
A sea foam mustache adorns their small face,
As they groove to the rhythm, at their own pace.

Jellyfish twirl, a ball of fine art,
With tentacles waving, they steal every heart.
Under the stars, laughter is the key,
In this watery realm, we're all wild and free!

Canvas of Sunset Dreams

The sun starts to paint the sky hues of fun,
While crabs hold a meeting, deciding to run.
In pink flip-flops, they march down the way,
To catch the last rays of a glorious day.

Seagulls are laughing, they spot a beach hat,
Worn by a tourist, asleep, what of that?
They steal it with flair, such a cheeky delight,
As the waves watch in glee, it's a comical sight.

A couple of starfish debate at their post,
Who's the best dancer? They choose the one boast.
But every time one star leaps for the chance,
He trips on the sand, then they all start to prance.

The horizon giggles, a ticklish affair,
Turning from orange to lavender air.
As night descends, it's a laughter parade,
In the canvas of twilight, we happily wade.

Echoing Footsteps on the Isle

Footprints in sand lead a curious trail,
As crabs take the lead on their own little sail.
Tickling toes, they scuttle and tease,
Claiming the shoreline with utter ease.

A picnic spreads out—sandwiches fly!
When gulls swoop in, oh my, oh my!
A donut rolls off like a bowl in the stream,
While laughter erupts, it's a comical dream.

Seashells gossip about the day's share,
They whisper and giggle, making quite the flair.
A clam tells a joke, but it's under his breath,
Yet the laughter erupts at the thought of his theft!

As shadows grow long, the fun must not end,
With echoes of joy, on the beach they blend.
In every step taken on this sandy isle,
We find joy in the laughter, and memories to smile!

Chorus of Seaglass Shards

On sunny days the seagulls squawk,
They steal my fries, oh such a shock!
With salty wings and beady eyes,
They swoop on by, much to my surprise.

The beach ball bounces, kids all cheer,
But wait! There's sand right in your beer!
A crab takes off with my beach hat,
I chase him down, imagine that!

Flip-flops fly like boomerangs,
As I chase the tide, my laughter clangs.
With every splash and sandy slip,
I find the joy in every trip.

Oh, life's a dance on the sunlit shore,
Where laughter echoes, forevermore.
So grab a drink, let's dance around,
In this funny place, pure joy is found!

Verses in the Breeze

Breezy days make kites take flight,
But not my sandwich, oh what a sight!
A gull swoops down, I shout, "Hey dude!"
He takes my lunch in a sneaky mood.

The waves come in with a sloppy kiss,
As I try to balance, can't help but miss.
I trip and tumble, all in good cheer,
Waves laugh with me, that's why I'm here.

Seashells talk in whispers low,
They gossip about the tides that flow.
With each crash, there's a punchline found,
In nature's humor, we're all spellbound.

Oh, what a theater, this sandy stage,
Where nature's quirks never age.
So let's enjoy this funny spree,
In verses shared, just you and me!

Ballad of the Hidden Cove

In a cove where weird things hide,
You'll find a fish with a crazy stride.
He wears a hat and sings a tune,
Under the light of the gleaming moon.

There's laughter in the playful tide,
Where seaweed dancers twist and glide.
A starfish chuckles at my flop,
While bubbles rise, it just won't stop!

Crabs throw parties in the deep,
While I try not to make a peep.
They've got moves that I've never seen,
And I'm stuck here, just a marine bean.

So join the fun, come take a look,
These sea creatures write the best book!
In this hidden cove, such joy we'll find,
With giggles and grins, we'll unwind!

Sonnet of Forgotten Shores

On the shores where laughter tends to drift,
Old shoes and seaweed together shift.
Waves tease the sand with a playful kiss,
While crabs scuttle by, not wanting to miss.

The sun winks down, a mischievous tease,
As wind whispers secrets through the palm trees.
Forgotten toys from summers of yore,
Lie half-buried, waiting for more.

With each new wave, a fresh joke unfolds,
A fresh fish arriving, with tales to be told.
Seashells giggle as they chat away,
In this world of wonder, we sing and play.

So here's to the shores where laughter brings,
Together we dance, oh the joy it sings!
With every beach day, we set our hearts free,
In the warm, funny hug of the sea.

Echoes in the Breeze

A parrot tells tales of lost socks,
While crabs dance around in their tiny frocks.
Seagulls squawk jokes that are quite absurd,
As the beach ball rolls away, it's been disturbed.

Sunbathers snore loudly, what a funny sight,
As waves crash and giggle, their laughter feels right.
A coconut tumbles and lands on a toe,
With a plop and a bop, it starts quite the show.

The flip-flops are flying, all over the sand,
Chasing a breeze, on a joy-filled command.
The sandcastles melt in the heat of the noon,
Like ice cream forgotten, they're gone way too soon.

But laughter is echoing, round every nook,
While toes dip in water, come take a look!
With the sun shining bright, what a wonderful tease,
Join the parade of giggles, let's dance in the breeze!

Waves of Solitude

A dolphin wears goggles, he's ready to race,
While shells hold the gossip from each little place.
The beach ball is bouncing, it's lost in the tide,
While sandcastles tumble, it's chaos inside.

A starfish is posing, a true little star,
While fish in a school are practicing ballet at the bar.
Seashells whisper secrets no one can hear,
While seaweed does yoga, quite zen, it feels clear.

The sun shines a spotlight, a shimmer so bright,
As flip-flops are flying, oh what a sight!
The waves joke about, they splash and they play,
While crabs do the cha-cha, what a fine day!

In the rhythm of laughter, we all find our beat,
As the tides roll on in, and the heat's a repeat.
With every chuckle, and all the fun gained,
Life in this solitude feels wonderfully strained!

Heartbeat of the Shores

The sand shimmies brightly like a shimmering grin,
As the seagulls give chase to the sneaky wind.
A hermit crab fumbles, with a shell that's too big,
While dolphins just giggle, and dance the sea jig.

The surfboards are surfing, the surfers just fumble,
While the octopus giggles, causing quite the jumble.
Each wave has a rhythm, a tune that it sings,
While driftwood gets carried, on imaginary wings.

The sun takes a bow, then cracks a wide smile,
While children with buckets run mudslides a mile.
The heartbeat of shores plays a tune ever sweet,
With laughter and joy, it's a jubilant beat!

Laughter and waves dance, a comical pair,
As the tides carry wishes to float in the air.
Every splash tells a story, each ripple a rhyme,
In this funny paradise, let's cherish our time!

Secrets Beneath the Palms

The palms sway gently, they whisper their schemes,
As lizards debate on the best sunbeams.
A coconut rolls down, with a knowing little grin,
While the sun lounges low, and encourages sin.

Underneath the shade, where the weird critters talk,
A crab shares his secrets on an imaginary walk.
The turtles doze off, dreaming of pies,
As sunbathers snore, with snickers and sighs.

The breeze brings a chuckle from the tropical trees,
While children build kingdoms, with buckets and seas.
Each palm leaf conceals a tale oh so funny,
As the day drifts onward, feeling warm like honey.

When the moon rises up, bringing sparkling delight,
The secrets get louder, and the shadows invite.
With laughter as currency, joy floats in waves,
In the realm of the palms, where the fun never craves!

Poetry of the Swell

Waves laugh and dance, oh so spry,
Seagulls gossip as they fly.
Fishermen's tales with a wink and a grin,
Casting their lures, hoping for fin.

A crab in a tux, he struts with flair,
While starfish snooze without a care.
Surfers tumble in a splashy show,
Even the breeze can't help but blow!

Turtles race to the beach for a sun,
While flip-flops squeak, oh what fun!
Sandcastles rise, then get knocked down,
By giggles and splashes, a merry sound.

At dusk, the bonfire lights the scene,
With marshmallows toasted, sticky and keen.
The ocean hums an offbeat tune,
As we dance 'neath a winking moon.

Mandolin Under Moonlight

Strumming strings beneath the stars,
A playful tune floats by, oh so far.
Fish jump high, in a curious leap,
While crabs tap dance, in silence they creep.

The moon grins wide, in a bright, silly way,
As lizards join in for a night of play.
With every note, the coconuts sway,
Even the shadows want to stay.

Mermaids chuckle in the gentle tide,
As seaweed sways like a goofy slide.
Flip-flops flare with every beat,
We're giggling now, can't feel our feet.

Waves carry laughter, each sound a treasure,
Even the night seems to leap with pleasure.
A mandolin croons to the ocean's hush,
As moonbeams twinkle in a playful rush.

Whirlwind of Palm Leaves

Palm leaves flutter, a wild parade,
Dancing in breezes, a leafy charade.
Coconuts wobble with laughter so grand,
While ants throw a party in the warm sand.

The parrot cackles, a jokester it seems,
As children race after their wobbly dreams.
Beach balls zoom like comets in flight,
While sandpipers hop in sheer delight.

With every gust, the laughter surges,
As the ocean plays its fun-filled urges.
Shells giggle softly, secrets they keep,
While flip-flops tango in a clumsy leap.

Crabs join in, waltzing with pride,
In this whirlwind of joy, they joyfully glide.
We laugh and we play as the sun starts to fade,
Creating sweet memories, laughter displayed.

A Dreamer's Cove

In a nook where dreams softly swell,
We share our stories, oh, what a tell!
With laughter like waves that crash and roll,
Funny ideas bubbling, tickling the soul.

Seashells are trumpets, announcing our fun,
As sandy spirits join us, one by one.
Tickled toes are a game tonight,
Launching laughter into the starry twilight.

The moon's a jester, with a big, silly grin,
As fireflies waltz, letting joy seep in.
Each wave a giggle, each ripple a sigh,
In this cozy cove where silly dreams lie.

So grab a seashell and sing a tune,
Let your worries drift in the ocean's croon.
In A Dreamer's Cove, laughter won't cease,
Where merriment reigns and hearts find peace.

Gentle Cradle of the Surf

Waves splash and dance on golden sand,
Seagulls laugh, with fish in hand.
A rubber duck floats, a pirate's dream,
While crabs hold court, plotting scheme.

The sun gets tired, it starts to yawn,
Flip-flops abandon, the beach is drawn.
Sandy toes wiggle, in funny delight,
As waves rush in, for a ticklish fight.

Children build castles, with moats and walls,
While dad claims victory, in a sandball brawl.
Laughter echoes, under the sky so blue,
As seaweed capes are donned, a hero crew.

At dusk, fireflies dance, in a wobbly flight,
Marshmallows roast, with jittery delight.
And crickets join in, a comedic show,
As we all hum along, to the beachside glow.

Fragments of the Floating World

A rubber duck sails, dreams in its eyes,
With a tiny hat that takes to the skies.
Octopuses juggle, in a watery play,
While fish try to dance, but float away.

A whale tells jokes, in a deep booming voice,
His punchline leaves even dolphins with choice.
Seashells gossip of mermaids so fair,
While starfish just sit, plotting their hair.

The tide rolls in, like a cheeky old friend,
Bringing lost toys for the fun to extend.
Kites tangle high, in a wind-blown affair,
As laughter erupts in the salty sea air.

Sandy googly eyes, on a beach ball queen,
With a crown made of shells, she reigns so serene.
Under the moon, the beach becomes wise,
In its twilight glow, each creature just sighs.

Twilight Waters and Beyond

Frogs in bowties hold a dance on the shore,
While turtles slip by, with a leisurely snore.
The moon spills secrets, upon the waves' crest,
As starlight giggles, that's simply the best.

Pineapple umbrellas sway in a breeze,
Where laughter skips, and worries freeze.
Crabby performers give a comedy show,
While fish buy tickets, hoping to grow.

The night wears pajamas, comfy and bright,
As sandcastles melt in the soft fading light.
Glow-in-the-dark turtles dance in the dark,
While waves whisper tales, of a bright, silly lark.

Picnics of seaweed and jelly-filled jars,
Rumors of mermaids flying to Mars.
The ocean hums softly, a whimsical tune,
As night strolls on, beneath a playful moon.

Shimmering Paths Under Stars

Under twinkling stars, fish wear cool shades,
They gossip 'bout tides and the best ocean parades.
Lobsters as butlers, serve seaweed fine,
While dolphins take selfies, smiles combined.

Across the waves, a surfboard takes flight,
As giggles rise high, in the calm of the night.
A snail races by, with a gleam in its eye,
Waving at starfish, they cheer as they fly.

Floating on clouds made of cotton candy,
The entire tide joins, it's fun, not too dandy.
Seagulls play tag, in a dizzying chase,
While clams clap along to the rhythm of grace.

Painted shells glimmer, like laughter in air,
With every wave crash, there's fun everywhere.
Beneath sparkling skies, where dreams come to play,
The ocean spins stories, in a magical way.

www.ingramcontent.com/pod-product-compliance
Lightning Source LLC
Chambersburg PA
CBHW072134070526
44585CB00016B/1668